BY ANN BRAYBROOKS · ILLUSTRATED BY MICHAEL SUND

With special thanks to David Saffron at The Puzzle Zoo, Santa Monica, California. And thanks to Yoni Shoshani for sharing his artistic vision with us.

Published by Price Stern Sloan, Inc.,
A member of The Putnam & Grosset Group, New York, New York.

Printed in the United States of America. Published simultaneously in Canada.
Library of Congress Card Number: 94-67449

ISBN 0-8431-3890-4

First Printing

1 3 5 7 9 10 8 6 4 2

Contents

What is POG™?

It's fun, fresh, wacky, and wild. It's a simple game that kids are playing all over the U.S.

It's also called TRŌV™, SkyCaps™, Bottle Caps, Milk Caps, Caps, Flips, and Disks, depending on who you talk to.

Whatever it's called, the basic game is easy to play. Two players stack round cardboard caps on a flat surface. Then they take turns trying to flip over the caps with a heavier, thicker round disk, called a *slammer* or a *kini*. If the kids are playing for points (called *funs*), they add up the disks that land face up. If they're playing for keeps (called *keeps* or *realsies*) . . . oops, they can lose their caps.

Besides playing with POGS™, kids are collecting and trading them. Why? Because a lot of the caps look outrageous. They're bright, colorful, and they show images of everything from cars to cartoon characters, movie stars to monsters, famous athletes to funky designs, and the names of sports teams, schools, and businesses.

With the caps in this kit, you can start your own collection. And with the slammer, you can play right away.

So have fun, and slam on!

POG™ and POGS™ are registered trademarks of the World POG Federation™.
TRŌV™ is a registered trademarks of TRŌV™ USA, Inc.
SkyCaps™ is a registered trademark of Aegis Entertainment, Inc.

A Brief History

If you didn't have any games or toys at home, what would you do? You probably wouldn't sit there and twiddle your thumbs. You'd make up games of your own.

That's what kids did in the 1920s and 1930s, when lots of families didn't have money to spend on toys. In those days, kids had to invent their own games by using their imaginations and the objects around them.

Milk came in glass bottles then, and the bottles were sealed with cardboard caps. Kids saved the caps and made up the game that came to be known as Milk Covers (which makes sense!).

Over the years, the game became less popular, especially when dairies stopped delivering milk to homes in glass bottles. But a Hawaiian woman named Blossom Galbiso never forgot it. When she became a guidance counselor at an elementary school on the island of Oahu in Hawaii, she taught the game to her students. She had seen them playing war games on the playground and thought it would be better for them to play something less violent.

Niihau
Oahu
Kauai
Maui
Molokai
Lanai
Kahoolawe
Hawaii

That was in 1991. By that time, milk cartons had replaced milk bottles, so kids played with the cardboard seals from juice bottles instead. The most popular seal came from the Haleakala Dairy on the island of Maui and was found on the bottle containing Passion fruit-Orange-Guava juice (POG™—get it?).

In Hawaii, the cap craze spread from Oahu to the other islands. Soon, schools and businesses began to print their own caps. Schools printed caps with the school name or mascot on the front to raise money, and businesses used the caps to promote a company or product. Local artists also got in on the act, and some of their caps are among the most prized.

It wasn't long before the game spread to California, then the rest of the U.S. Today, kids are still flipping over it. They're collecting, trading, and playing with caps that feature every design you can dream of. They're also using their imaginations to invent new games.

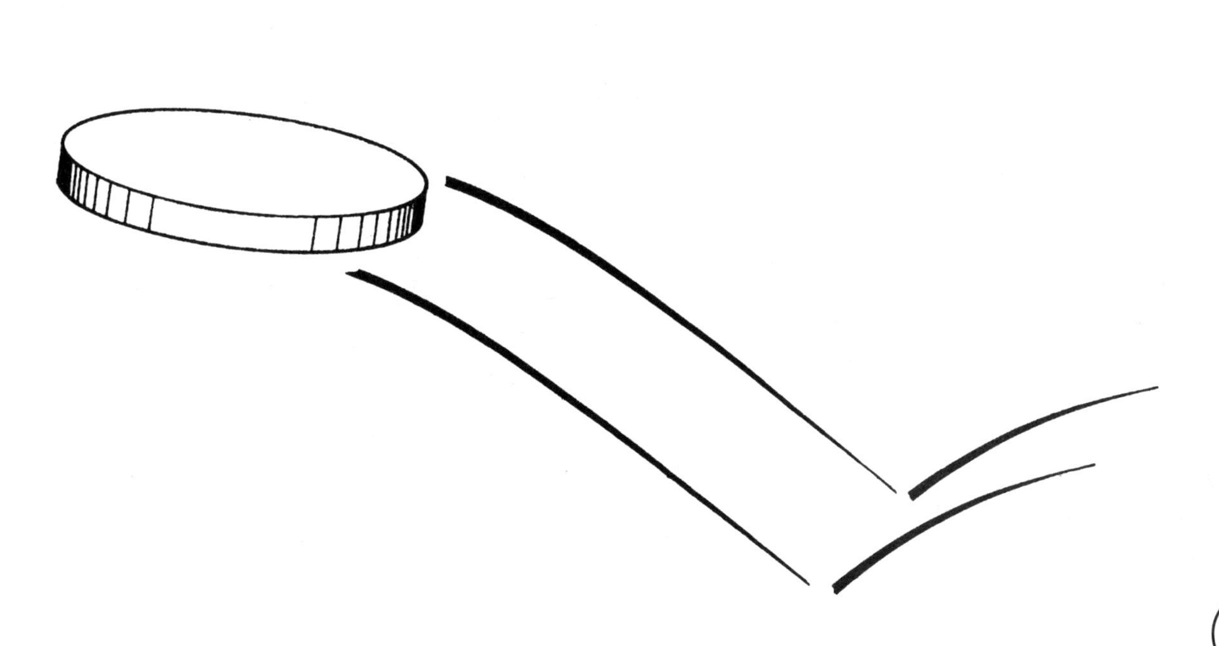

Hints

1. Use the caps in this kit to play the game. If you want to start a collection, save a few of your favorite caps and keep them in a safe place.

2. If you lose your slammer, you can easily make another one by gluing three or more caps together.

3. Play only with plastic slammers, and save the metal ones for your collection. A plastic slammer is less likely to harm someone or put a dent in a wood table or other soft surface. If you have a combination slammer (a metal slammer enclosed in two plastic slammers), you should also save it for your collection.

4. Always play on a hard, flat surface, such as a table or level cement. Don't play on floors or tables made out of materials that can be damaged. If you like, you can buy a playing board. They're round and flat and can be found at many stores that sell caps.

5. To keep the game fun, play for points and not for keeps. (If you play for keeps, you may lose your favorite caps!) A scoresheet and pencil will help keep the totals straight. (See page 11).

6. During school hours, keep your caps in your backpack or another safe place. If you have any questions about your school's cap policy, ask your teacher.

7. After playing the games in this book, make up some of your own!

Who Slams First?

You've found a friend who's eager to play. How do you determine who goes first?

Here are a few ways:

1. Flip a coin. While the coin is in the air, have your friend shout "heads" or "tails."

2. Toss a cap like a coin. Art-side-up equals "heads." The plain side, or side with the manufacturer's name on it, equals "tails."

3. Toss two caps and call a match or odd pair. While the caps are in the air, ask your friend to yell "same" or "different."

4. Play Paper Scissors Stone.

• Each player holds one fist shut.

• At the same time, players raise their closed fists up and then lower them. On the downward movement, both say either, "One" or "Paper."

• While continuing to keep their fists shut, players move their fists up and down again, this time saying either, "Two" or "Scissors."

• Again, both players raise and lower their closed fists, saying either, "Three" or "Stone."

• Upon saying "Three," or "Stone" players make one of three signs: two fingers opened in a V represents scissors; a closed fist indicates stone; a hand held open with the palm up is paper.

• Scissors wins over paper (because scissors cut paper). Stone wins over scissors (because stone blunts scissors). Paper wins over stone (because paper can wrap around the stone).

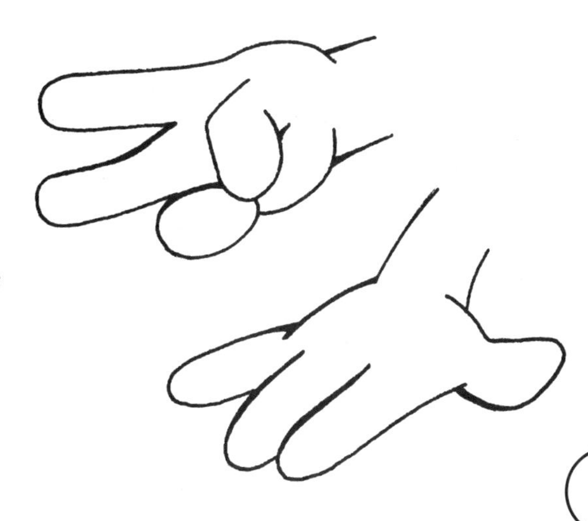

• For Paper Scissors Stone to be fair, both players must raise and lower their fists at the same time. They must also open their fists at the exact same moment, so neither player gains an advantage by seeing what sign the other player makes.

Slamming and Jamming

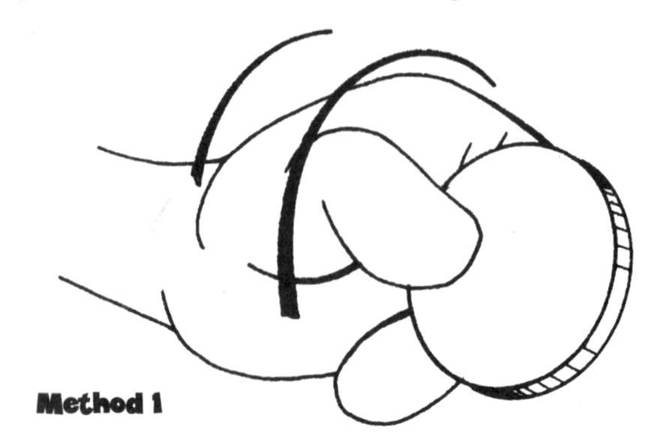
Method 1

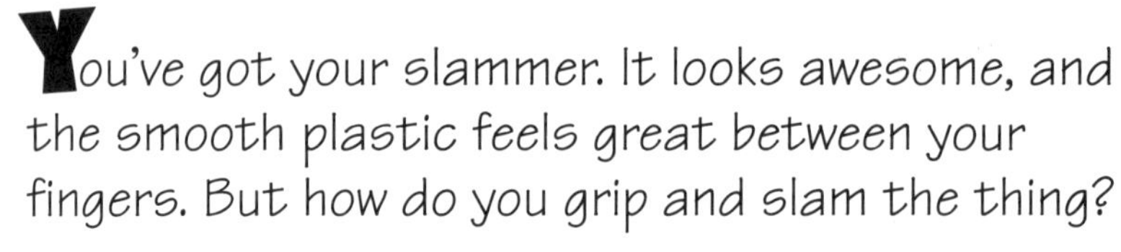

You've got your slammer. It looks awesome, and the smooth plastic feels great between your fingers. But how do you grip and slam the thing?

Make up your own way, or use one of these:

Method 1

1. Balance the slammer on your index finger and middle finger, then grip the slammer on top with your thumb. (Kids under seven can use three fingers—the index, middle, and ring fingers.)

2. Quickly rotate your wrist (while still holding the slammer) so your thumb is on the bottom and your fingers are on top.

3. Toss the slammer at the stack as hard as you can, making sure your fingers don't touch the stack.

Method 2

1. Grip the slammer with your thumb on the bottom and your fingers on top.

2. Instead of rotating your wrist, just throw the slammer down at the stack of caps.

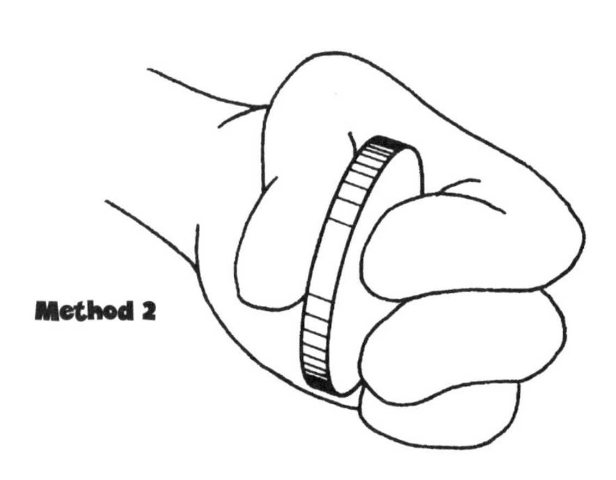
Method 2

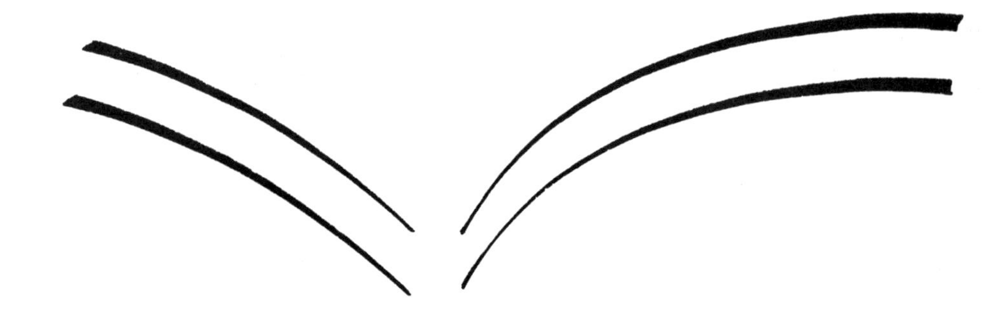

Method 3

1. Balance the slammer on your index and middle fingers, but don't use your thumb.

2. Quickly rotate your wrist and slam down.

Method 4

Grasp or "pinch" the rim with your thumb and index finger, keeping the slammer flat, then slam down.

Method 5

Pinch the rim with your thumb and index finger, but hold the slammer upright, then slam down.

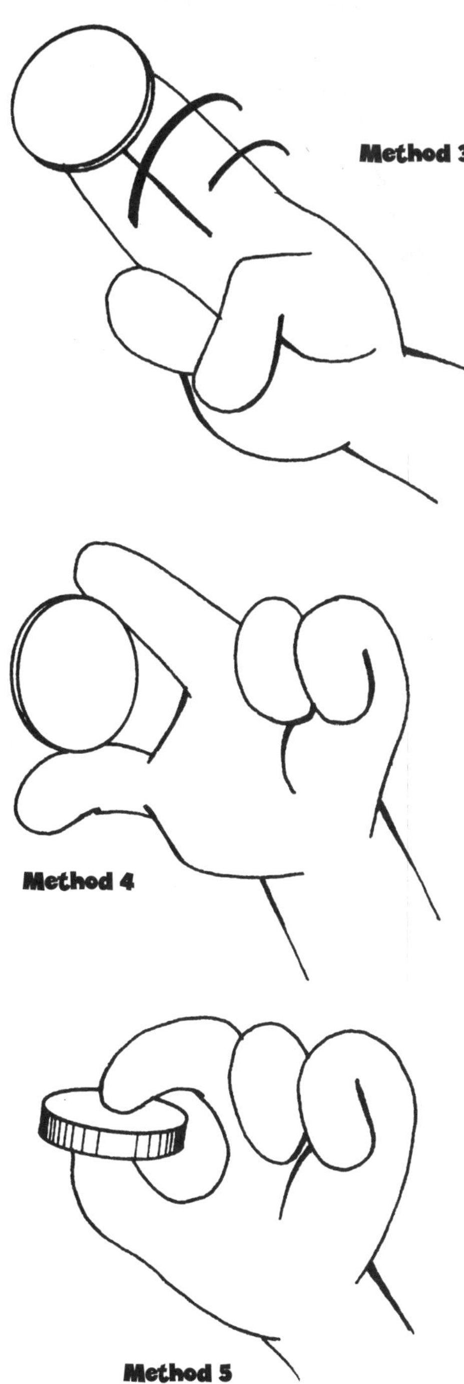

Now try out these slamming techniques:

- Throw the slammer like a Frisbee™, flinging it at the stack from the side.
- Use any of the gripping methods above and aim for the middle of the stack.
- Aim for the edge of the stack and see what happens.
- To steady your aim, touch the top cap in the stack with your slammer, then lift and slam down.

Remember, speed and coordination are everything!

How to Play

Now, after some history, hints, and handwork, it's time to play the game! Be sure to have the following:

- at least two players (one besides yourself)
- four or more caps per player
- one slammer per player
- a flat surface
- a scoresheet
- a pencil

1. On a flat surface, each player stacks an equal number of caps face-down. (Placing the caps face-down protects the art from getting dented or scratched.) Each player should contribute an equal number of caps—at least four or five. One player can stack his or her caps on top of the other player's, or players can alternate putting caps on the stack one by one.
2. Players determine who goes first by using one of the methods on page 7.
3. Players call out any special rules. (See pages 12–13.)
4. The first player slams his or her slammer at the stack, making sure to release the slammer just above the caps (before it touches the top cap).

5. For every cap that lands face-up, that player gets a point. (If playing for keeps, the player gets to keep the caps.) Remove the face-up caps from the stack, and write the points on the scoresheet.

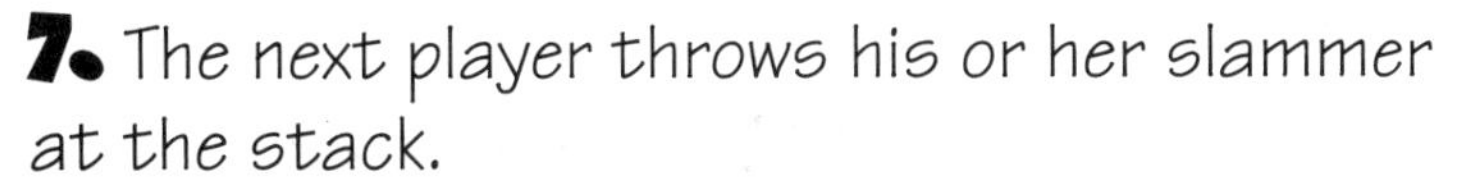

6. The player restacks the remaining caps so the next player can slam.

7. The next player throws his or her slammer at the stack.

8. Players take alternate turns slamming until all the caps have been flipped over.

9. The player with the most points (or caps) wins!

A note about the point system: While many of the original games involve playing for keeps, and winning caps and slammers, we suggest you play for funs, or points, instead; therefore, we've come up with the following scoring system:

1 cap = 1 point

1 slammer = 5 points

1 empty tube or case = 10 points

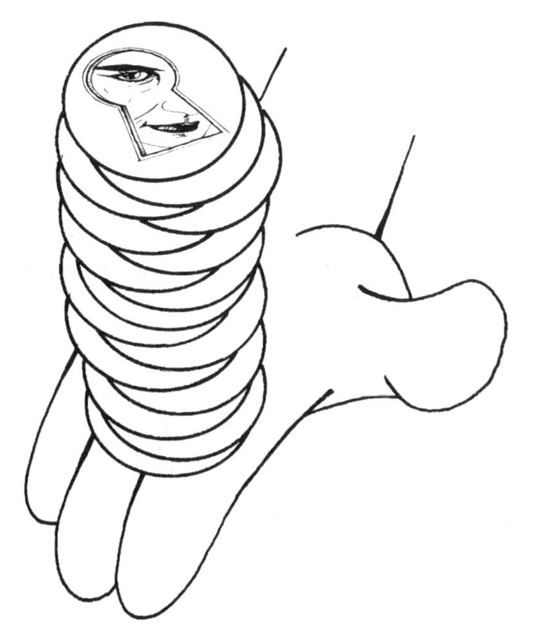

Rules

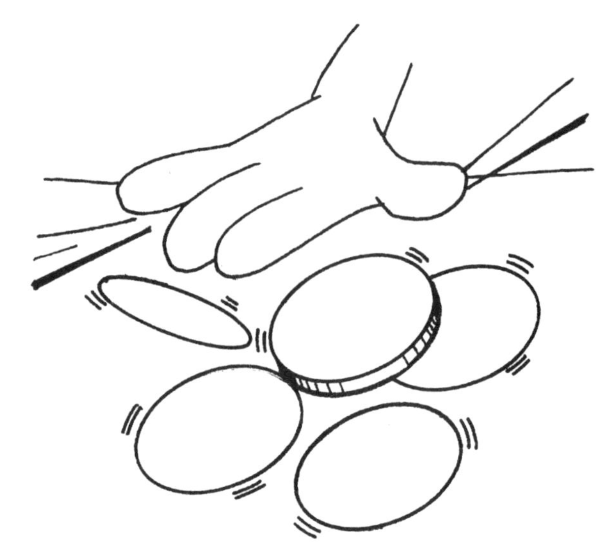

There you are, watching your opponent throw her slammer, when all of a sudden she slaps her hand on the table. All the caps flip over except one, and she gets more points than she would have if she hadn't pounded the table. Hey, wait a minute! Is this fair?

It's fair if two players don't agree on the rules before starting a game. Of course, you can always make up your own rules, but here are a few you may want to call out at the beginning:

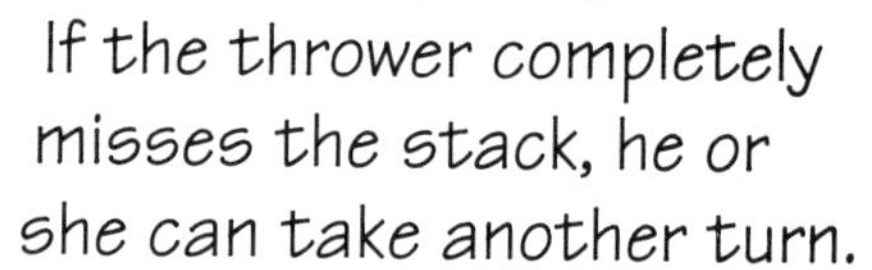

"Miss-no-count:" If the thrower completely misses the stack, he or she can take another turn.

"No-out-hitter" or "No doctors:" At any time during the game, another person cannot substitute for a player.

"Safety:" A player can add his or her own caps to the stack. This is usually done when the stack is short (just a few caps) and the player is afraid that he or she won't be able to flip any over. If a player calls "Safety" and none of the caps flip over, he or she is allowed to remove the caps he or she added to the stack. Of course, the next player can also do the same thing.

"No Safeties:" Players are not allowed to call "Safety" at any point during the game. If "No Safeties" is not called at the beginning of the game either player can shout "Safety" before a turn.

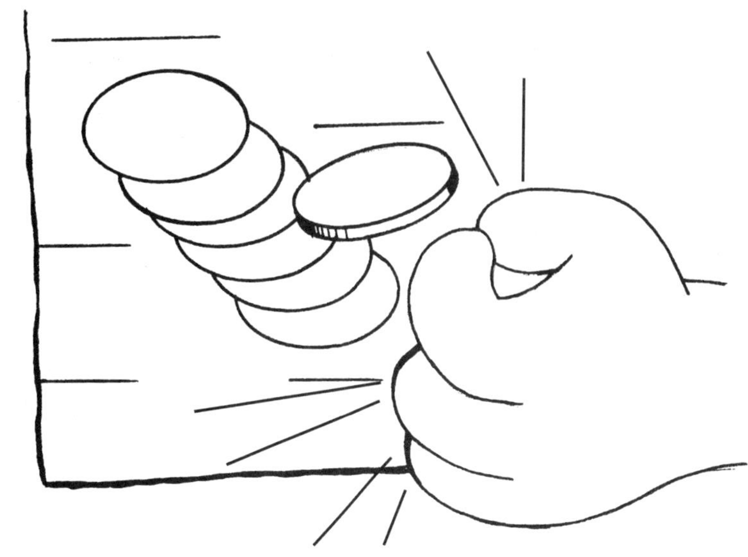

"No slaps:" Players cannot hit the playing surface as follow-through (trying to make more caps flip over).

"No tippies" or "No pigtails:" Players cannot use the edge of the slammer to flip over the last cap in the stack, like in tiddlywinks.

Here are some other things to think about:

1. Ideally, caps should be the same size, weight, and thickness. This also goes for slammers; however, since there are so many different types of slammers on the market, it's OK for each player to use a different kind as long as both agree to it at the beginning of the game.

2. For a "fair hit," a player's fingers must not touch or hit the stack. The slammer should always be released just before it hits the caps.

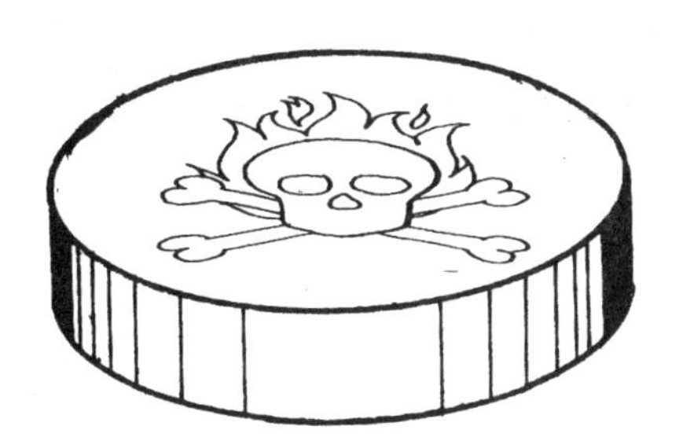

More Games to Play

After you learn the basic game, you'll be eager to try some variations. Although the rules often vary—from player to player, state to state—you can use these as a starting point, then make up your own versions.

However, as mentioned earlier, always make sure that you and your opponent are following the same rules. At first, you may want to keep this book nearby for reference.

Also, if you don't have a particular slammer, ask the other player if you can substitute another.

The important thing is to have fun, improve your slamming skills, and remain friends with your opponent!

ABCs

1. Tournament players use special slammers with a bomb* on them to play this game, but you can play with any slammer as long as it is OK with the other player.

2. Player One puts a cap face-up on the playing surface. Then the same player puts a cap face-down on top of the first cap.

3. Player Two puts two caps face-down on top of the stack.

4. Players take alternate turns slamming.

5. If one player flips over the top three caps without flipping over the bottom cap (so all are facing up), that player gets 5 points (the equivalent of a slammer) and wins.

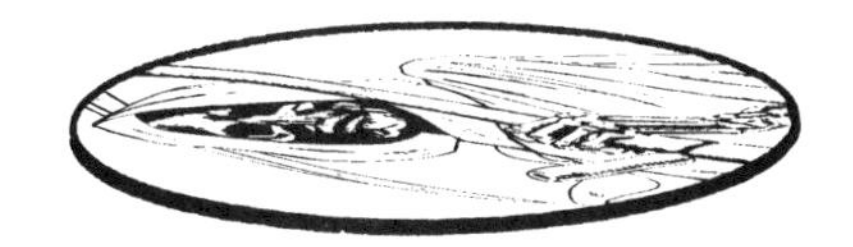

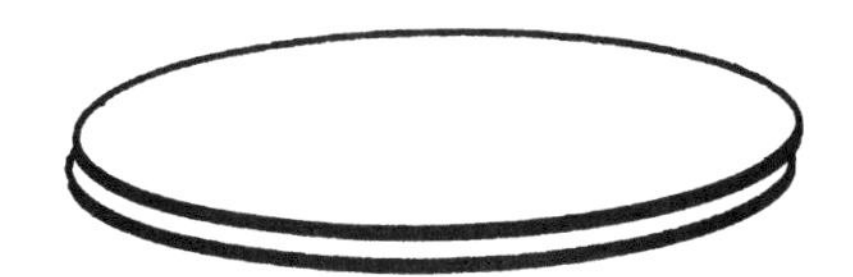

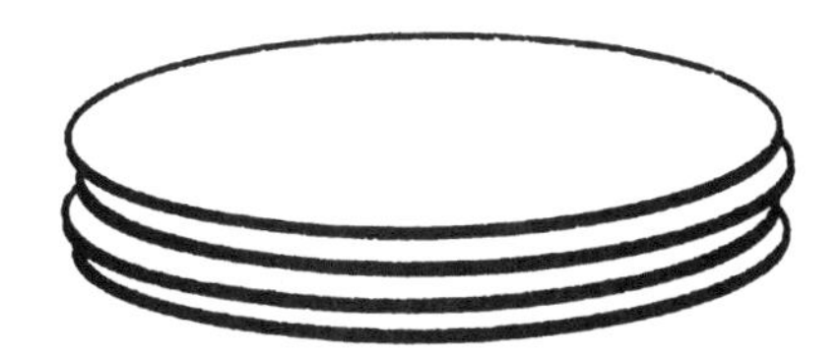

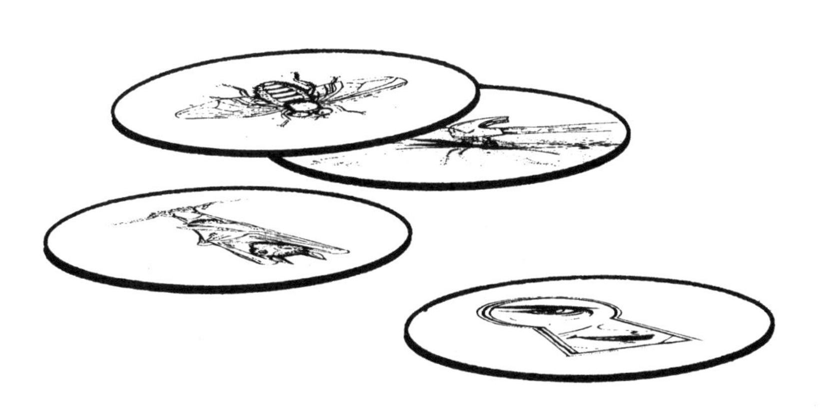

*Bomb slammers are produced by dozens of different manufacturers. STRIKE ZONE produces a PRO STRIKER™ (not shown here) that has a bomb on it.

Annihilator

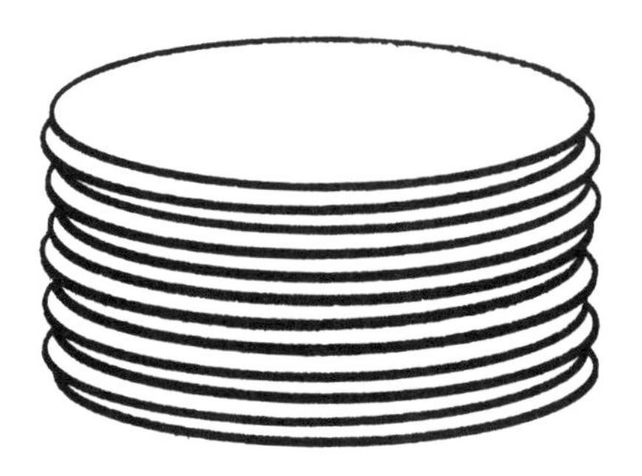

1. Tournament players use special metal slammers to play this game, but you can play with any slammer as long as it is OK with the other player.

2. Players stack as many caps as they want face-down. (Each player must contribute an equal number of caps.)

3. Players alternate taking turns slamming until one player flips over all the caps in one slam.

4. That player wins and gets a point for each cap in the stack, plus 15 points (the equivalent of his or her opponent's slammer and tube).

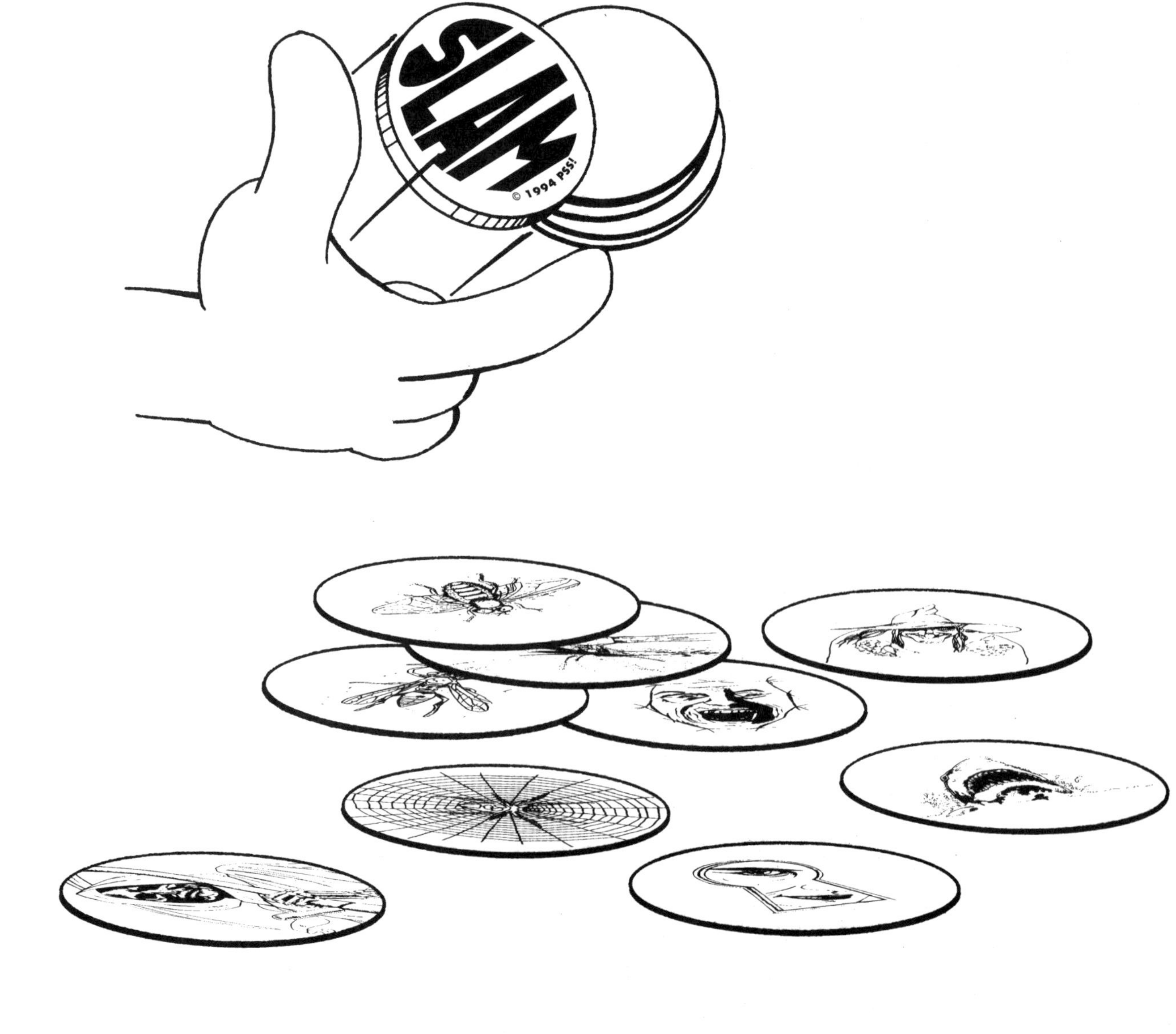

Black Magic

1. Tournament players use a special Crusher™* slammer to play this game, but you can play with any slammer as long as it is OK with the other player.

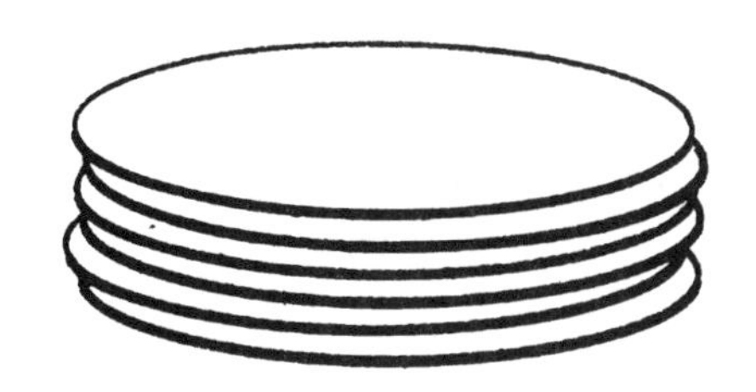

2. Each player contributes three or more caps to the stack, for a total of six or more caps. (Each player must contribute an equal number of caps.) Stack the caps face-down.

3. The first player taps the top cap with his or her slammer, then lifts the slammer and yells, "Black Magic" while slamming.

4. The goal is to split the original stack into two stacks of caps (still face-down) plus flip over the middle cap so that it is face-up.

5. If this happens, the player places the face-up cap between the two stacks so that all are touching. Then he or she taps the cap in the middle with the slammer and says "Black Magic" again.

6. The player gets 1 point per cap plus 10 points (the equivalent of two slammers) for the winning total.

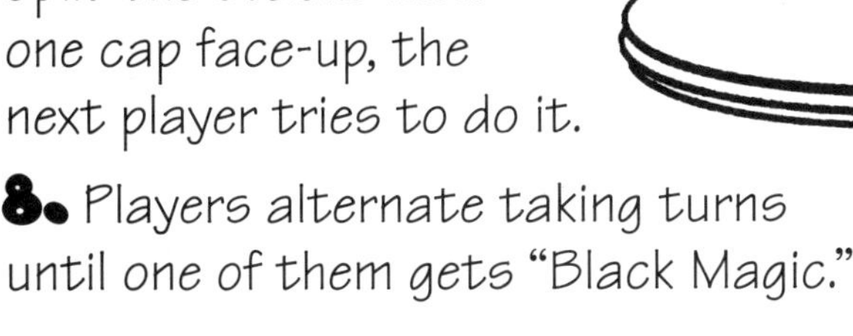

7. If the player does not split the stacks with one cap face-up, the next player tries to do it.

8. Players alternate taking turns until one of them gets "Black Magic."

*Crusher™ is a registered trademark of Harshaw Enterprises.

Crisscross

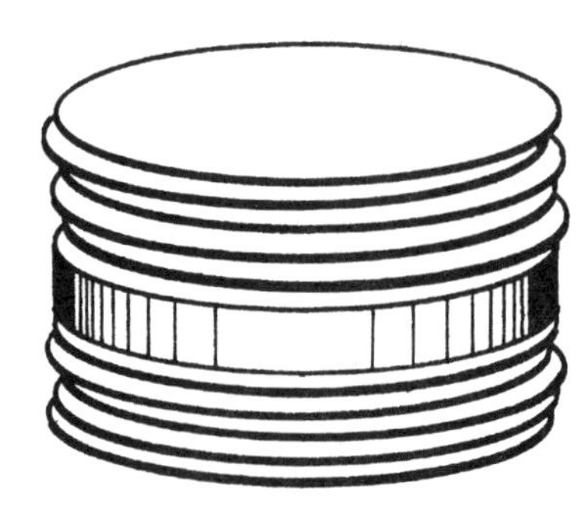

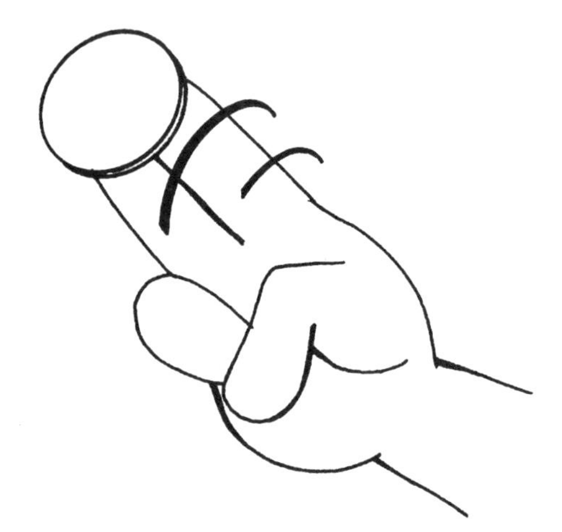

1. Tournament players use special bad to the bone* slammers to play this game, but you can play with any slammer as long as it is OK with the other player.
2. Each player contributes five or more caps so that there are 10 or more caps in the stack. (Each player must contribute an equal number of caps.) The caps should be placed face-down.
3. Player One places a slammer face-down in the middle of the stack.
4. Player One holds a slammer with the index and middle fingers (but not the thumb) and slams.
5. The goal is to flip over the slammer and the entire stack of caps. If the slammer and all the caps don't flip over, the next player takes a turn.
6. When a player manages to flip the slammer and all the caps in one slam, that player yells, "Freeze!"
7. That player gets 1 point for each cap and 5 points for the slammer.
8. The caps are restacked with the slammer in the middle, and the next player gets a chance to flip over all the caps.
9. If the player doesn't flip over all the caps, the player who did and yelled, "Freeze," can now shout, "Defreeze!" That player wins the game and gets another set of points for each cap and the slammer.

*Bad to the bone slammers usually have muscled, grumpy-faced people on them; they are produced by dozens of different manufacturers.

Eight Ball

1. Tournament players use special eight ball* slammers to play this game, but you can play with any slammer as long as it is OK with the other player. One player should also have a holographic cap.

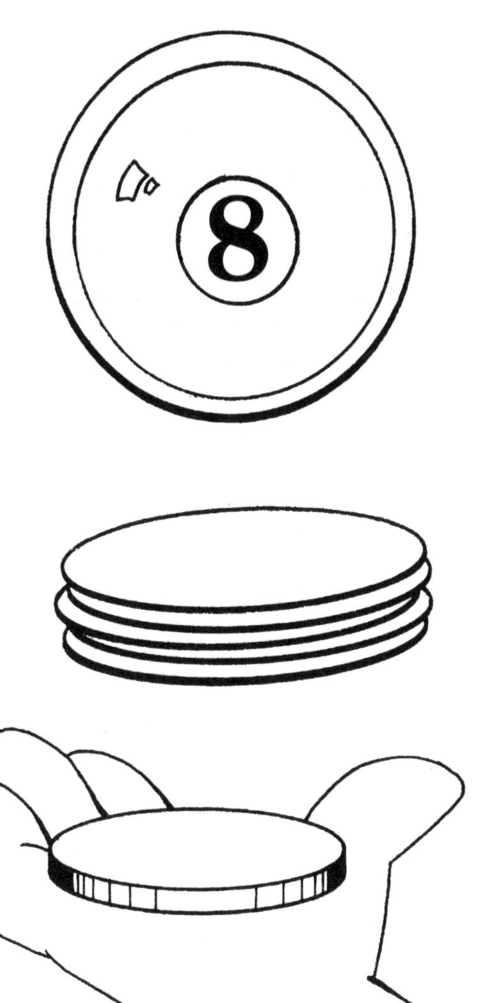

2. To play, stack the holographic cap plus four or more caps face-down in a stack.

3. Player One holds a slammer in the palm of his or her hand, rotates the wrist, and slams, aiming for the middle of the stack.

4. The goal is to flip over all the caps in the stack plus make the slammer land underneath all the flipped-over caps. When a player manages to do this, he or she taps the top of the flipped-over caps with a finger and calls "Eight Ball." That player, the winner, gets 5 points.

5. Players alternate taking turns until one of them gets "Eight Ball" and wins.

*Eight ball slammers are produced by dozens of different manufacturers.

The Leveler

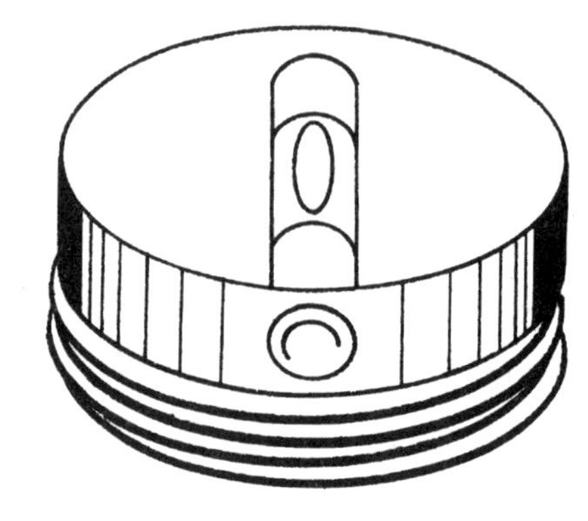

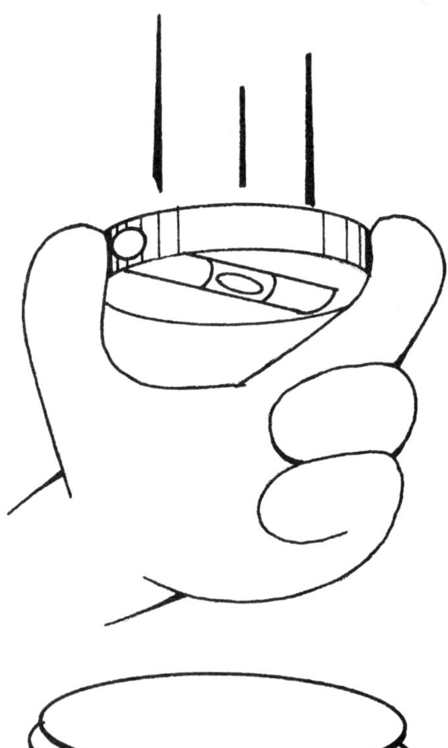

1. This game must be played with a special slammer. At least one of the two players must have a clear plastic slammer with a leveling tube in the middle.*

2. Players stack as many caps as they want face-down. (Each player must contribute an equal number of caps.)

3. Player One places the slammer on top of the stack so that it is perfectly level. (There should be only one liquid bubble inside the leveling tube.)

4. That player then lifts the slammer and slams the stack.

5. Both players quickly examine the slammer. If the bubble has split into two bubbles, the player that threw the slammer gets 1 point for each cap the other player has and 5 points for each slammer the other player has. For this game to be fair, both players should come to the playing surface with the same number of caps and slammers.

6. If the bubble has split into anything other than two bubbles, the next player goes.

7. Players alternate taking turns until one splits the bubble in two.

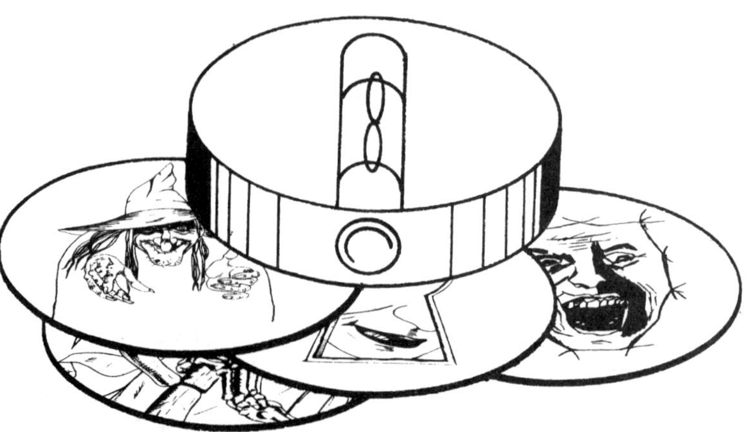

*These small, disk-shaped levels are actual carpentry and tiling tools that can be found at many home-improvement and hardware stores.

Poison

1. Tournament players use special Poison™* slammers to play this game, but you can play with any slammer as long as it is OK with the other player.
2. Players stack as many caps as they want face-down. (Each player must contribute an equal number of caps.)
3. Player One slams the stack with his or her slammer.
4. The goal is to hit the stack without flipping over any of the caps. If this happens, the player slides his slammer in a circle around the stack, then taps the slammer and shouts, "Poison!" That player gets a point for each cap in the stack.
5. Players alternate slamming until one of them gets "Poison" and wins.

*Kygar Entertainment has a special Poison™ slammer (not shown here) which is a registered trademark.

Rainbow

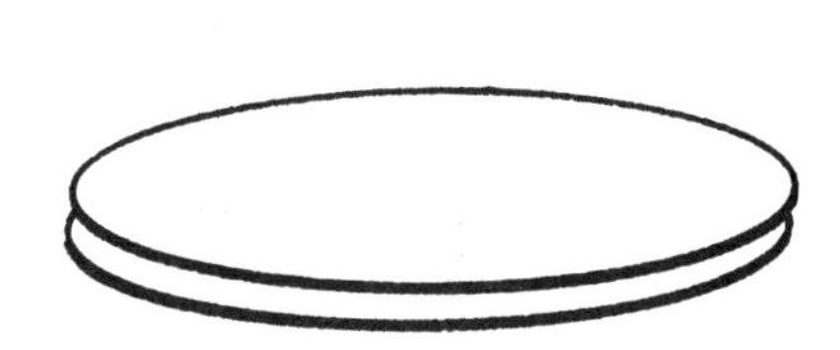

1. Tournament players use special slammers with the yin-yang* symbol on them to play this game, but you can play with any slammer as long as it is OK with the other player.

2. Each player contributes one cap.

3. Place the two caps in a stack face-down.

4. Player One holds his or her slammer by "pinching" it (holding it by the rim with the thumb and index finger). The player slams.

5. If that player flips over both caps, he or she gets 10 points (five times the two caps in the stack).

6. If the player does not flip over both caps, Player Two tries.

7. Players alternate taking turns until one of them flips over both caps and wins.

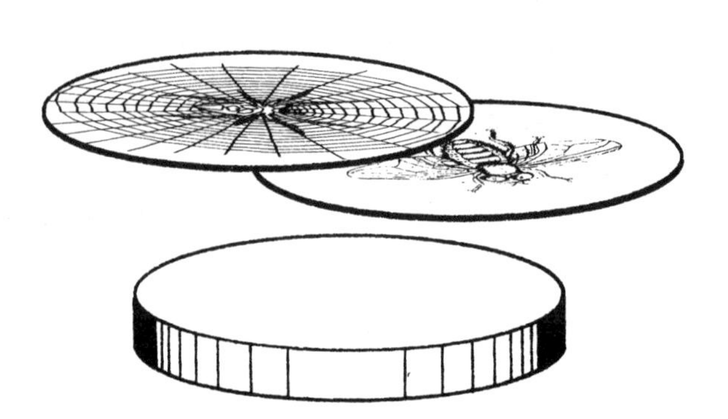

*Yin-yang slammers are produced by dozens of different manufacturers.

Scorpion

1. Tournament players use special slammers with a scorpion* on them to play this game, but you can play with any slammer as long as it is OK with the other player.

2. Players stack as many caps as they want face-down. (Each player must contribute an equal number of caps.)

3. Players alternate taking turns slamming until one player flips over all the caps in the stack except the bottom cap. (It's tough to do—but possible!)

4. The winner gets 1 point for every face-up cap plus 10 points (the equivalent of two slammers).

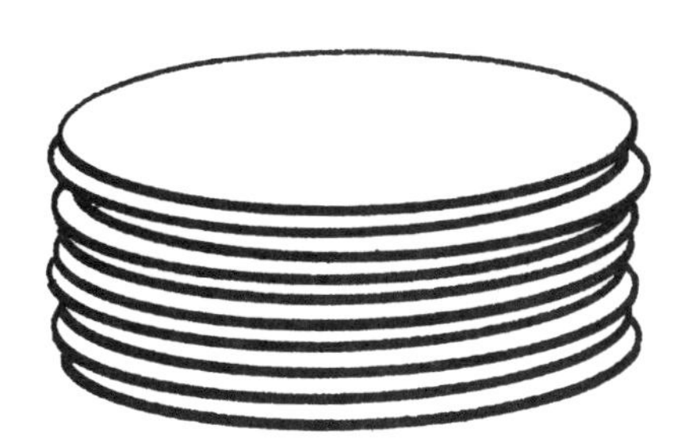

*Scorpion slammers are produced by dozens of different manufacturers.

Tornado

1. Tournament players use special slammers with a skull* on them to play this game, but you can play with any slammer as long as it is OK with the other player.

2. Each player contributes three caps to the stack. The caps (six total) should be placed face-down.

3. Players alternate taking turns slamming until one player flips over three or more caps.

4. The player who flips over three, four, or five caps wins the game and gets 5 points (the equivalent of a slammer).

5. However, if all of the caps flip over, the player does not get any points, and the game continues.

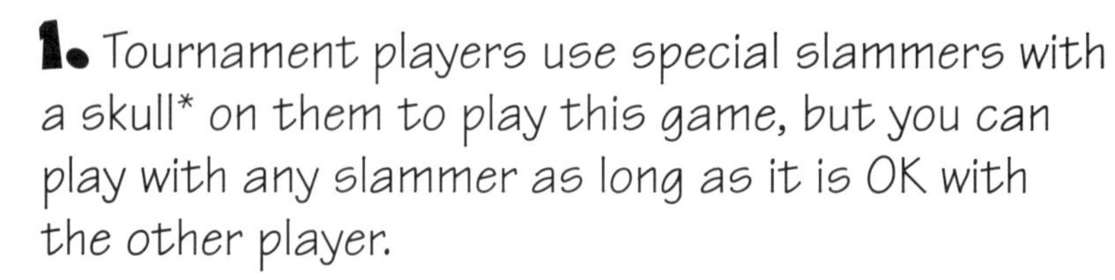

*Skull slammers are produced by dozens of different manufacturers.

Triplets

1. Tournament players use special super dominator* slammers to play this game, but you can play with any slammer as long as it is OK with the other player.

2. One player (either one) stacks three caps face-down.

3. Players alternate taking turns slamming until one player flips two caps so that they land face-up on either side of the cap that remains face-down.

4. The winner taps the slammer with a finger and says, "Dominator." The winner gets 7 points. (If you are playing for keeps, the winner grabs all three caps and hands them to his opponent. The loser must then give the winner 10 caps of the winner's choice.)

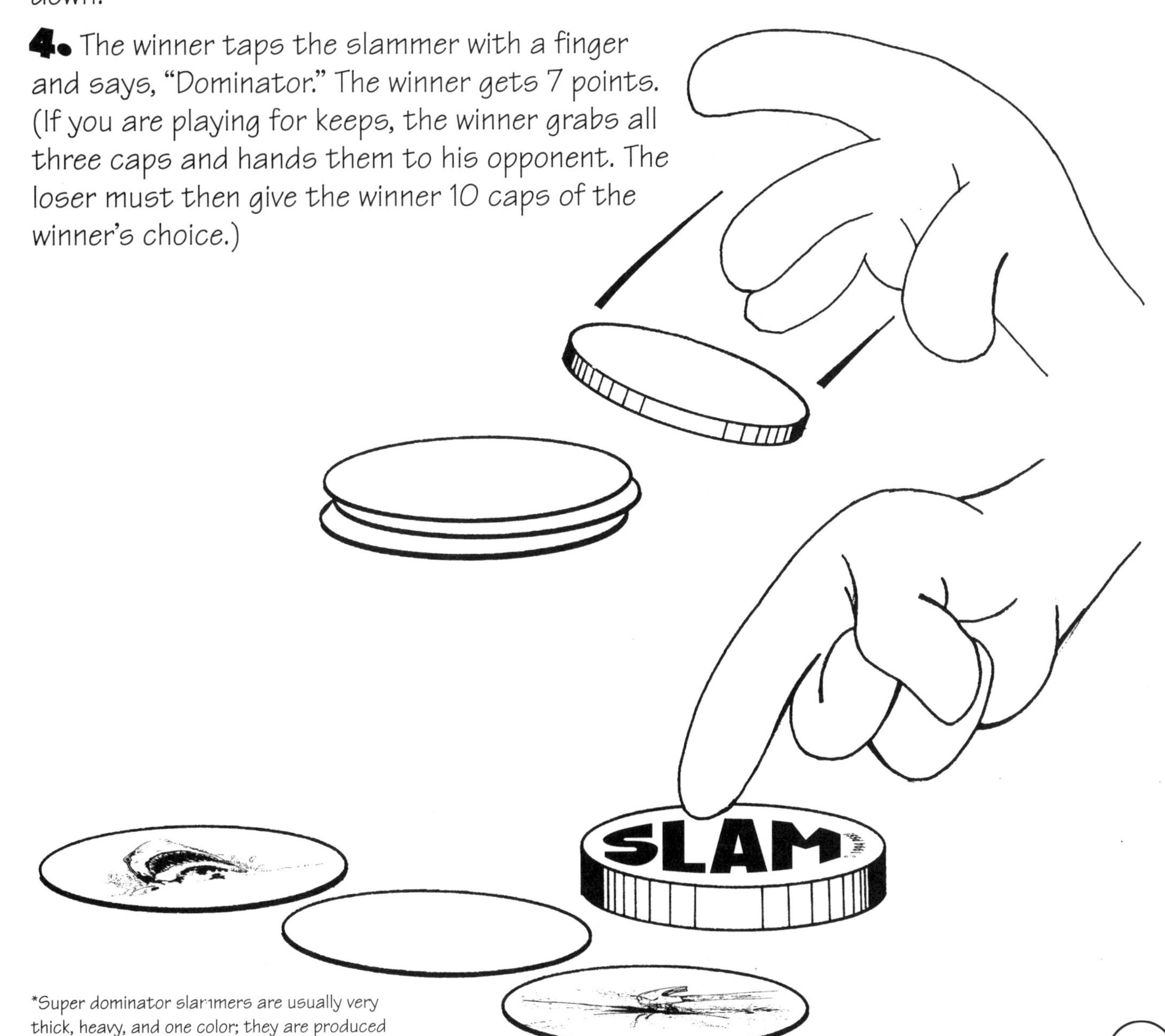

*Super dominator slammers are usually very thick, heavy, and one color; they are produced by dozens of different manufacturers.

Venom

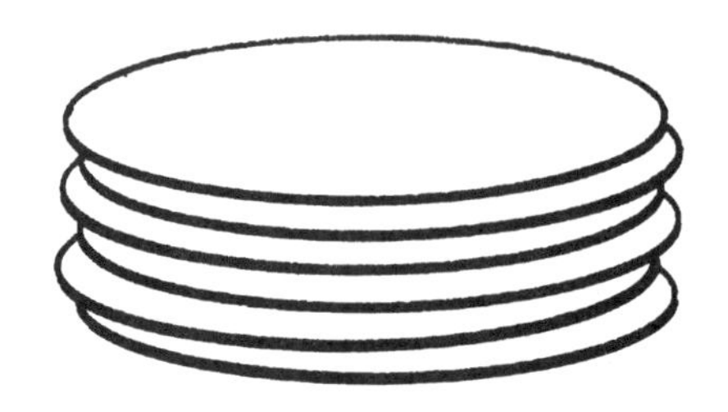

1. Tournament players use special venom* slammers to play this game, but you can play with any slammer as long as it is OK with the other player.

2. Players stack as many caps as they want face-down. (Each player must contribute an equal number of caps.)

3. Players alternate taking turns slamming.

4. For every cap that a player flips over, that player gets two times the number of points. (This is what's known as a doubling game.) For example:

1 cap = 2 points

2 caps = 4 points

3 caps = 6 points

5. However, if a player flips over the entire stack, he or she gets only one point for each cap. (The player cannot double the number of caps in the stack.)

6. Players play for as long as they want, keeping their individual scores.

7. When they stop, the player with the most points wins.

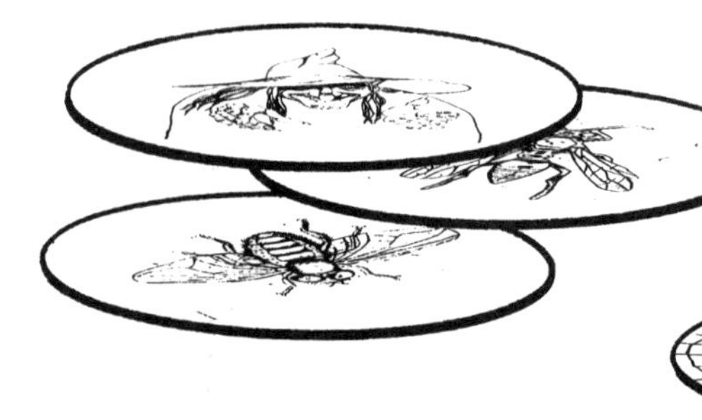

*Venom slammers usually have a snake on them and are produced by dozens of different manufacturers.

Making Up Your Own Games

Now that you're a slam champ, try inventing your own games. Use the games in this book for inspiration, or make up other ways of playing with caps and slammers.

Here are a few ideas to get you going. Use them alone, or combine them to create something new and exciting:

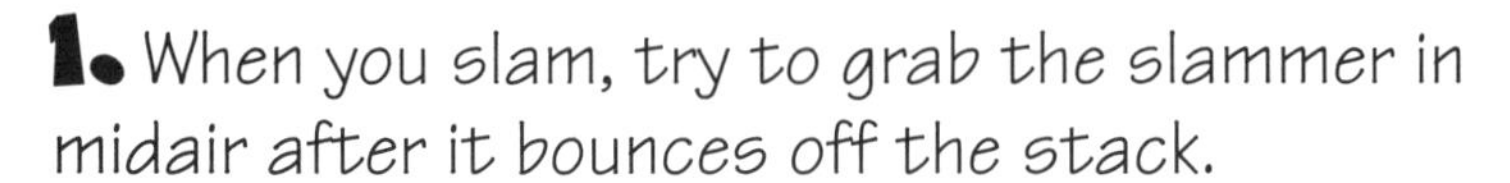

1. When you slam, try to grab the slammer in midair after it bounces off the stack.

2. Build the tallest stack of caps that you can without the stack sliding over, then slam.

3. Play with two stacks of caps placed side-by-side.

4. Play a version of tiddlywinks by using a slammer to flip caps into a small cup or jar.

5. Before you slam, call out the number of caps you think will flip over. (You can call this game "Prediction!") A player gets points when he or she calls out the correct number.

6. Play a version of shuffleboard by sliding the slammer across a flat surface so it knocks a cap into a designated area.

7. Play a version of tic-tac-toe using caps.

How to Set Up a Tournament

In some areas of the country, you'll find tournaments sponsored by different manufacturers and organizations, and you should definitely check them out. To raise money for a good cause, you may want to help organize a tournament at your school or with your favorite community group. You can even organize a fun, unofficial tournament at home with friends.

For super-casual home tournaments, you don't need anyone to supervise; however, if you'd like someone to oversee the competition, either do it yourself (without playing) or ask another non-player to keep score and referee.

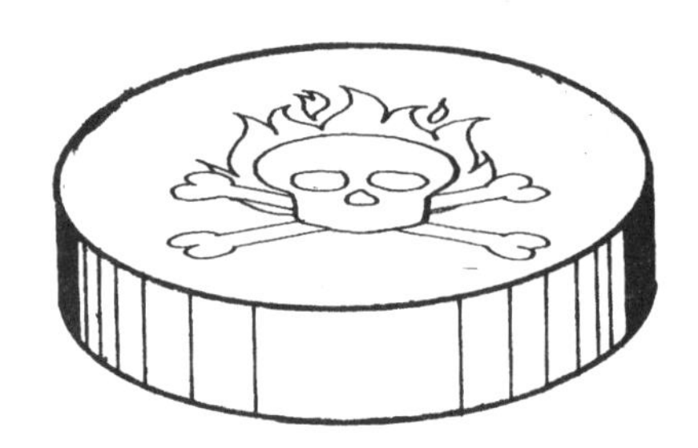

Use the following guidelines for home play, and expand them for a fund raiser:

1. Have at least four players present.
2. Make sure that each player has a slammer that is equal in size, weight, and thickness.
3. Divide the players into an even number of pairs such as two or four, not three or five.
4. Ask players to put a specific number of caps face-down in a stack. (Some tournaments use an even number of caps, others use seven, still others 11—you decide what works best for you. Any number that can be slammed is fine.)

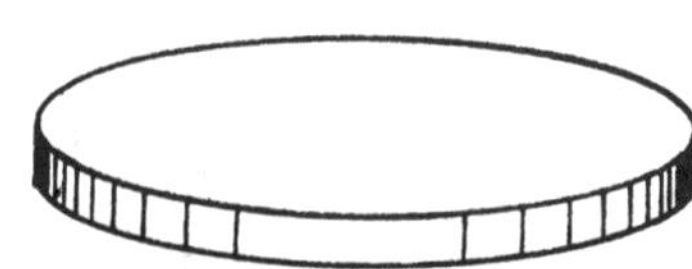

5. Before anyone starts, explain the rules. Tell players how many caps they need to flip over to win a game. (For example, a player must flip four out of seven caps to win, or four out of 11, or six out of 11—again, you decide!)

6. For each game, players determine who slams first by using one of the methods on page 7.

7. When players are ready to start, shout "Ready, Set, Slam!"

8. At the same moment, the first player in each pair slams his or her slammer at the stack.

9. Players alternate taking turns slamming until one player in each pair flips over the designated number of caps.

10. The winners of each pair advance to the next round, and the game is repeated. Use a chart like the one below to show the results of the tournament.

11. The winner of all the rounds wins the tournament.

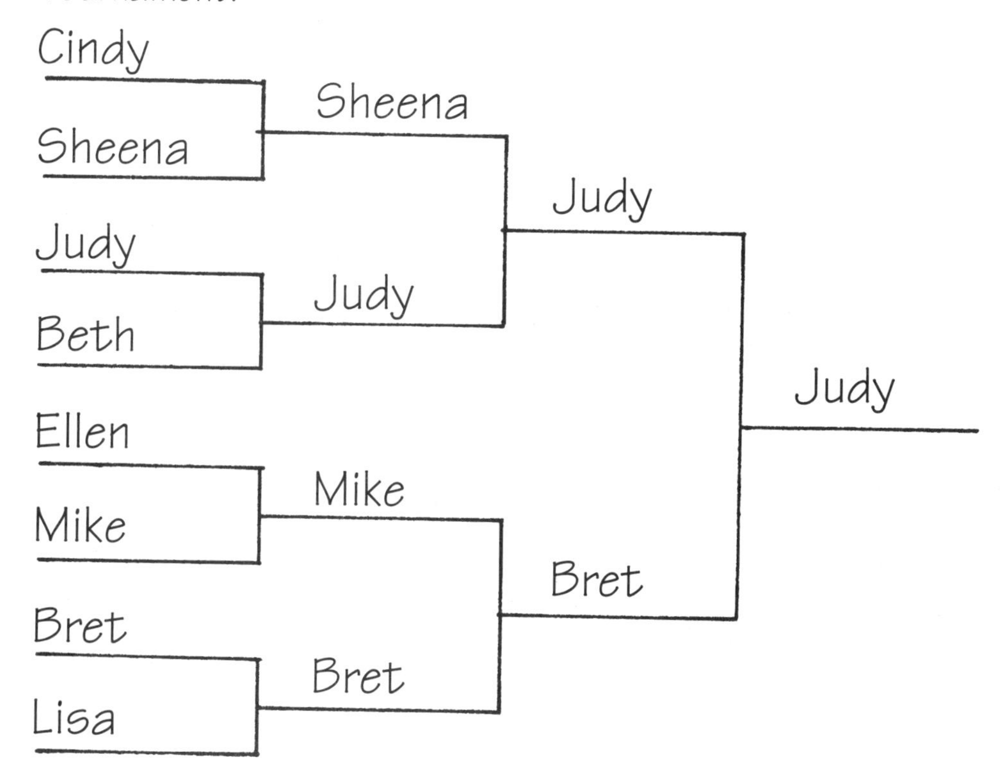

Collecting Caps

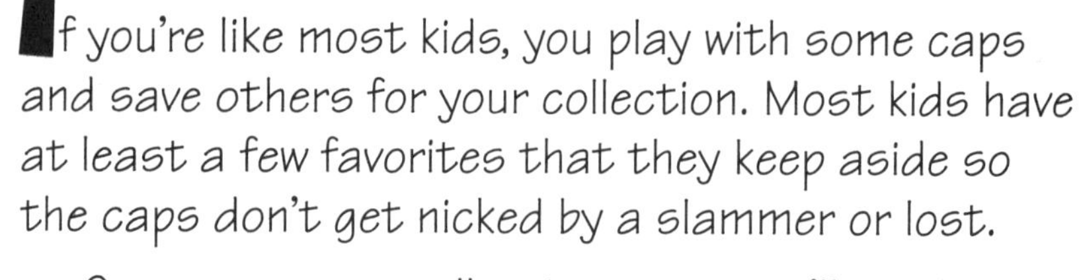

If you're like most kids, you play with some caps and save others for your collection. Most kids have at least a few favorites that they keep aside so the caps don't get nicked by a slammer or lost.

Once you start collecting caps, you'll need to store them somewhere. Consider keeping them in plastic tubes with snap-on tops or in clear plastic slide-holder sheets that can be placed in a binder. (You'll find the tubes, sheets, and binders in many stores that sell caps.) If you can afford to pay more and spend time looking, you can also purchase clear acrylic holders that have special cap compartments.

Serious collectors should research what kind of plastic holder is best to store caps in. (Some plastics contain chemicals that can ruin cardboard over time.) One cap expert suggests buying holders made out of acrylic because these materials don't break down the way other plastics do.

If you keep your caps in a cardboard box, make sure the cardboard is acid-free. All caps—no matter how they are stored—should remain dry and not be exposed to light for long periods of time. (Light can cause the ink on older, more delicate caps to fade.)

If you're interested in learning more about collecting, attend a cap or trading card show in your area. Or try doing research in the library or contacting the various cap manufacturers. They may be able to give you a list of the different caps they print, as well as information about collecting.

Soon, you'll learn who makes what, how much it's worth (one cap was sold for over $100!), and how far you want to get into collecting!

Trivia

• "Menkos" or "Menkins," a game similar to caps, has been played in Japan for hundreds of years.

• The original POG™ juice cap from the Haleakala Dairy has a pucture of a furry red animal called a "poglodyte" riding a surfboard.

• The "original" caps were manufactured for Hawaiian dairies by a company in Canada called STANPAC. Each cap was wax-coated and had a small pull-tab with a staple in it. The tab allowed juice drinkers to easily remove the cap from the bottle.

• TRŌV™, the cap manufactured by TRŌV™ USA, stands for "treasure trove."

• The Royal Hawaiian Milk Cap Company printed a limited-edition set of four caps—in 24-karat gold!

• Due to the popularity of caps in Hawaii, they were once referred to as "Hawaiian money."

Cap Talk

This list of terms should keep you cap-tivated!

cap: a cardboard disk, about the size of a silver dollar, used for playing caps

disk: another word for cap

doctor: a player who substitutes for another player in the middle of a game

funs: a game of caps in which points are totaled and caps are returned to their original owners at the end of the game

hitter: another word for slammer

keeps: a game of caps in which the player gets to keep all the caps he or she flips over, including those placed in the stack by his or her opponent

kini: the Hawaiian word for slammer

out-hitter: another word for doctor

pigtails: flipping over the last cap in a stack by tipping the cap on the edge with a slammer, like in tiddlywinks

pounder: another word for slammer

realsies: another word for keeps

safety: adding caps to a short stack. Usually done when a player thinks the stack is so short that he or she might not be able to flip any over.

scoop: to flip over, or win, the entire stack of caps in a game

slam: to throw a slammer at a stack of caps

slam board: a large, round board with a flat surface used for playing caps

slammer: a heavy, thick disk, usually made of plastic, used to hit a stack of caps

slaps: hitting the playing surface to make more caps flip over

striker: another name for slammer

tippy: another word for pigtails